DEREK JETER'S
ULTIMATE BASEBALL GUIDE
★ 2015 ★

By Larry Dobrow

Illustrated by Damien Jones

LITTLE SIMON JETER CHILDREN'S

New York London Toronto Sydney New Delhi

JETER CHILDREN'S

An imprint of Simon & Schuster Children's Publishing Division

1230 Avenue of the Americas, New York, New York 10020

First Little Simon paperback edition February 2015

Copyright © 2015 Jeter Publishing   9623

LITTLE SIMON is a registered trademark of Simon & Schuster, Inc., and associated colophon is a trademark of Simon & Schuster, Inc. For information about special discounts for bulk purchases, please contact Simon & Schuster Special Sales at 1-866-506-1949 or business@simonandschuster.com. The Simon & Schuster Speakers Bureau can bring authors to your live event. For more information or to book an event contact the Simon & Schuster Speakers Bureau at 1-866-248-3049 or visit our website at www.simonspeakers.com.

Cover designed by Dan Potash   Interior designed by Angela Navarra and Chani Yammer

Manufactured in the United States of America 0115 BID   10 9 8 7 6 5 4 3 2 1

ISBN 978-1-4814-2318-2   ISBN 978-1-4814-2332-8 (eBook)

In order to publish this book for the start of the 2015 baseball season, it was necessary to prepare it during the course of the 2014 baseball season. Trades and changes in statistics and other baseball data might have occurred since completion of the manuscript, and some of this data might not be included in the book.

A LETTER FROM DEREK JETER

Dear Readers:

From being a huge baseball fan as a kid to playing in the Major Leagues, **you could say I've learned a lot** about the game. And I couldn't think of a better way to share my passion than creating this ultimate baseball guide.

To me, baseball is a passion and a pastime. The passion has kept me playing through 20 seasons; the pastime fuels my fascination with the game. **Baseball speaks to the youth in our hearts,** no matter our age. This book is for those who love spending time with the game.

What is the oldest team? **Why are the Mets blue and orange?** Facts and stats, quotes and code, superstition and trivia—it's all here. We've even included menu fare. Baseball has a lot to offer.

Happy reading!

Derek Jeter

INTRO: HISTORY

There are a lot of theories about when baseball started. Some date the game back to 1842, while others say it goes back to the 1700s. Alexander Cartwright, who adapted it from the English game of rounders, is often referred to as the father of the modern game. A diamond-shaped field, equal distances between the 4 bases, and 3-out innings were among Cartwright's so-called Knickerbocker Rules.

The first documented game of baseball took place between Cartwright's Knickerbocker Base Ball Club of New York City and the New York Nine on June 19, 1846, in Hoboken, New Jersey. The Nine had its way with the Knickerbockers that day, winning by a score of 23–1.

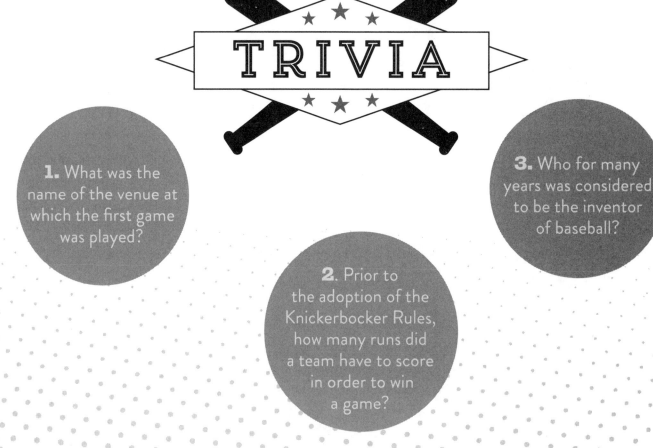

TRIVIA

1. What was the name of the venue at which the first game was played?

2. Prior to the adoption of the Knickerbocker Rules, how many runs did a team have to score in order to win a game?

3. Who for many years was considered to be the inventor of baseball?

(1. Elysian Fields)

(2. 21)

(3. Abner Doubleday, a Civil War general who, historians eventually proved, had next to nothing to do with baseball's creation.)

THE

TEAMS

EAST

AMERICAN
LEAGUE

2014 RESULTS

Baltimore Orioles	96–66
New York Yankees	84–78
Toronto Blue Jays	83–79
Tampa Bay Rays	77–85
Boston Red Sox	71–91

BALTIMORE ORIOLES
★ THE STREAK ★

The Orioles have won 3 World Series titles and returned to the playoffs after a tough stretch during the first decade of the 2000s. But as much as for anything else, the team is still defined by "the streak"—Cal Ripken Jr.'s 2,632 consecutive games played. It broke Lou Gehrig's record of 2,130 games—which had been thought to be unbreakable.

Ripken was inked into the starting lineup on May 30, 1982. He broke the record on September 6, 1995. He didn't take a day off until September 20, 1998. To put this into perspective, a streak of 324 consecutive games—2 straight 162-game seasons—is considered very impressive.

As much as for anything else, the Orioles are still defined by "the streak."

Cal Ripken is one of my personal baseball heroes!

TRIVIA

1. When Cal Ripken Jr. became eligible for the Hall of Fame, he appeared on 98.53% of the ballots cast, the third-highest number in history. What 2 players appeared on a higher percentage of ballots?

2. In what came to be known as one of the most lopsided trades in baseball history, pitcher Milt Pappas was sent to the Cincinnati Reds in exchange for which future Hall of Famer?

SECOND CALLINGS

Baltimore's Jim Palmer wasn't just one of the best pitchers in baseball history, winning 268 games and 3 Cy Young Awards as the American League's best pitcher. He also had one of the game's most unusual second acts. He served as a spokesman and model for Jockey underwear for nearly 2 decades. But his second career seems modest next to the ones enjoyed by . . .

Jim Bunning, U.S. Senator and Representative

His 224 wins, mostly with the Detroit Tigers and Philadelphia Phillies, secured him a spot in the Hall of Fame, but Bunning is probably better known as a politician. He served in the U.S. House of Representatives from 1987 to 1998, then served 2 terms as a senator.

Moe Berg, Spy

Although he played for 15 years, Berg was hardly a typical Major League catcher. A graduate of Princeton University and Columbia Law School, he spoke several languages. After his playing career ended, he served as a spy for the Office of Strategic Services during World War II, carrying out missions in Yugoslavia and Italy.

NEW YORK YANKEES

★ THE GOLD STANDARD ★

Since the franchise formally became known as the Yankees in 1913, it has succeeded to an extent unmatched in professional sports history. The team has won 27 World Series championships and 40 American League titles. Since the 1920s it has won at least 2 World Series titles in every decade, with the exception of the 1980s (during which the team still won a higher percentage of its games than any other team in baseball) and the 2010s.

Some of the game's all-time greatest players have been along for the ride: Babe Ruth, Lou Gehrig, Yogi Berra, Joe DiMaggio, Mickey Mantle, Whitey Ford, Thurman Munson, Reggie Jackson, Mariano Rivera, and of course Derek Jeter.

I used to have posters of Yankees on my bedroom wall as a kid.

TRIVIA

1. How many consecutive World Series games did the Yankees win between 1996 and 2000?

2. How many regular season and playoff games did the 1998 Yankees win, setting a single-season record?

TITLE TEAMS

If the St. Louis Cardinals won the next 15 World Series . . . well, they'd still trail the New York Yankees on the World Series leaderboard.

MOST WORLD SERIES TITLES

New York Yankees
27 wins (40 appearances)

St. Louis Cardinals
11 wins (19 appearances)

Oakland/Philadelphia Athletics
9 wins (14 appearances)

San Francisco/New York Giants
8 wins (20 appearances)

Boston Red Sox
8 wins (12 appearances)

Los Angeles/Brooklyn Dodgers
6 wins (18 appearances)

Cincinnati Reds
5 wins (9 appearances)

Pittsburgh Pirates
5 wins (7 appearances)

The Yankees have won 27 World Series.

TORONTO BLUE JAYS

★ DIVISION BLUES ★

The Toronto Blue Jays enjoyed substantial success in the late 1980s and early 1990s. They won 5 AL East titles in a 9-year stretch, along with World Series championships in 1992 and 1993. But since then, despite winning more games than they've lost, the Blue Jays haven't come especially close to reaching the playoffs. One possible reason for this is the division in which they play. Because of baseball's unbalanced schedule, the Jays play more games against AL East teams than they do against anyone else. And recently 3 of the 4 other AL East teams—the Yankees, Red Sox, and Rays—have fielded consistently strong teams.

TRIVIA

1. Which player hit the walk-off home run that clinched the 1993 World Series for the Blue Jays?

2. Which slugger hit a league-leading 54 home runs in his second season with the team, despite never having hit more than 16 in any previous season?

(1. Joe Carter)

(2. Jose Bautista)

THE
SUPERSTITIONS

Before completing a no-hitter on September 2, 1990, Blue Jays starter Dave Stieb came close several times. He lost no-hitters in the ninth inning 4 times, 3 times with 2 outs in the inning. Thus he was well acquainted with a long-standing baseball superstition: speaking of an in-progress no-hitter is a no-no. It's tradition for teammates to give the silent treatment to any pitcher flirting with a no-hitter and stay far away from him in the dugout.

Most of the game's most colorful superstitions, however, have been individually practiced:

Turk Wendell

chomped on 4 pieces of black licorice (not 3, not 5) as he pitched. Between innings he spit them out and then retired to the dugout, where he brushed his teeth.

Larry Walker

had a thing for the number 3, which manifested itself in his jersey number (33) and setting his alarm for 33 minutes past the hour. His wedding ceremony was called for 3:33 p.m. in the afternoon on the third day of November.

Wade Boggs

wouldn't leave the field following infield practice until he stepped on third base, second base, and first base, then touched the baseline and the coach's box. He also ate chicken before every game.

The Jays play more games against AL East teams than they do against anyone else.

TAMPA BAY RAYS

★ IF AT FIRST YOU DON'T SUCCEED... ★

Tampa Bay was awarded a baseball team in 1995 and started play in 1998 . . . and almost immediately made local fans wonder why they'd wanted a team for so long. In the team's first ten seasons, it finished last in the American League East 9 times. The other time? Next to last. But even as the 2007 Rays finished the season at 66–96, change was on the way. A new owner, Stuart Sternberg, had assumed control of the organization in 2005, and he attempted to do things differently, building around young players. In 2008 the changes finally showed up in the standings: the Rays won the AL East and advanced to their first-ever World Series (which they lost, to the Philadelphia Phillies). From then until 2013, the team finished with a winning record every season and won fewer than 90 games only once.

TRIVIA

1. What 2 teams did the Rays defeat in the 2008 American League playoffs to advance to the World Series?

2. Which Tampa Bay third baseman won Rookie of the Year after being called up to the Majors less than 2 years after he was drafted?

NUMBERS GAME

The Rays have a reputation for using every available statistical tool to make smarter, more forward-thinking decisions. But while advanced statistical analysis remains a relatively new development, teams have been keeping track of statistics for quite some time—since the mid-nineteenth century, when journalist and historian Henry Chadwick started writing his *Base Ball Memoranda*.

Chadwick is credited with devising statistical measures still used today, such as batting average and earned run average. Here's a brief list of baseball's big stats:

HITTING:

Batting average (BA)
The number of hits divided by at-bats

On-base percentage (OBP)
Times reached base (hits + walks + hit-by-pitch) divided by at-bats + walks + hit-by-pitch + sacrifice flies

Slugging percentage (SLG)
Total bases (1 for single, 2 for double, 3 for triple, 4 for home run) divided by at-bats

Runs batted in (RBI)
The number of base runners that score as a result of a batters' action, not including double-play groundouts and errors

PITCHING:

Earned run average (ERA)
(Total number of earned runs (does not count runs that score because of an error or passed ball) multiplied by 9) divided by innings pitched

Walks and hits per inning pitched (WHIP)
(Walks + hits) divided by innings pitched

Win
Game in which a pitcher was pitching when his team took the lead, and his team ultimately won the game. A starter must pitch 5 innings to qualify for a win.

BOSTON RED SOX
★ CURSE REVERSED ★

The story went like this: Red Sox owner Harry Frazee needed money to produce a Broadway show, so he sold his best player—Babe Ruth, who had set the single-season home run record in 1919—to the New York Yankees. The Red Sox over the next 86 seasons came close to winning a World Series multiple times. Unfortunately for them, they were "cursed" by this trade, which set the Yankees up for one of the most dominant eras in baseball history. The local media dubbed the Red Sox's bad luck "the Curse of the Bambino."

The curse ended in 2004 when the Red Sox were down 3 games to none in the American League Championship Series against the Yankees but then won the next 4 games. The team didn't stop there, sweeping the St. Louis Cardinals in the World Series to claim its first title since 1918. The Sox won again in 2007 and 2013.

The curse of the Bambino lasted for 86 years until the Red Sox won the World Series in 2004.

TRIVIA

1. Which Red Sox legend racked up 2,654 hits, 521 home runs, and nearly 3 times as many walks as strikouts, despite missing 3 seasons due to military service?

2. In what year did the Red Sox start playing their games in Fenway Park?

THE JUNIOR CIRCUIT

The American League is the younger of baseball's 2 leagues. It was formally created on January 28, 1901—some 25 years after the National League formed, which is why the American League is referred to as the "junior circuit." Ban Johnson, a onetime sportswriter, is credited with having brought the league together. Charter franchises included 7 teams that, to this day, still play in the American League:

Baltimore Orioles
(Not related to the current Baltimore Orioles)

Boston Americans
(Became the Boston Red Sox)

Chicago White Sox
(Same)

Cleveland Blues
(Became the Cleveland Bronchos, the Cleveland Naps, and the Cleveland Indians)

Detroit Tigers
(Same)

Philadelphia Athletics
(Became the Kansas City Athletics and then the Oakland Athletics)

Milwaukee Brewers
(Became the St. Louis Browns and then the Baltimore Orioles)

Washington Senators
(Became the Minnesota Twins)

AL EAST POP QUIZ

Now that you've aced the AL EAST, let's test your smarts! Score a single for 1 correct answer, a double for 2, and a triple for 3. How many runs can you score by the end of the book?

1. Which AL East team has won the most World Series titles?

2. What player broke Lou Gehrig's streak of consecutive games played?

3. During their first 10 seasons, how many times did the Tampa Bay Rays finish above last place in the division?

BUY ME SOME PEANUTS
AND
CRACKER JACK

(and tamales, and lobster rolls, and fresh fruit . . .)

In 2014, the average Major League Baseball game lasted longer than 3 hours for the first time—3 hours, 2 minutes, to be precise, and the average postseason game, prolonged by longer between-inning breaks, lasted nearly 24 minutes more than that. What does this mean to you, the game-attending fan? That you're likely going to want a snack or two to tide you over.

Stadium chefs and concessionaires have come a long way since the days when cold, rubbery hot dogs were the first and only item on the menu. Here are some of the league's tastier and more creative options, along with the stadiums in which one can find them:

BRATZEL DOG
(Busch Stadium, St. Louis)

A grilled bratwurst, but with a twist—a soft pretzel replaces the bun

CARNE ASADA FRIES
(Petco Park, San Diego)

This one is best described as a mathematical formula—thin french fries + ultimate nachos (thin-sliced steak + guacamole + cheese) - nacho chips = carne asada fries

THE SCHMITTER
(Citizens Bank Park, Philadelphia)

Born in a downtown Philly pub (and not named after Phillies great and Hall of Famer Mike Schmidt), this sandwich is a twist on the traditional cheesesteak. It adds salami, tomatoes, and a special sauce to the grilled steak, fried onions, and cheese.

STUGGY'S CRAB MAC 'N' CHEESE DOG
(Oriole Park at Camden Yards, Baltimore)

It is everything its name suggests—a hot dog overloaded with mac and cheese, plus lumps of crab meat—and yet so much more.

BURNT ENDS
(Kauffman Stadium, Kansas City)

If you attend a sporting event in Kansas City, you are going to eat barbecue. That's how it works.

CENTRAL

AMERICAN LEAGUE

2014 RESULTS

Detroit Tigers	90–72
Kansas City Royals	89–73
Cleveland Indians	85–77
Chicago White Sox	73–89
Minnesota Twins	70–92

DETROIT TIGERS

★ ROCK BOTTOM ★

The Tigers have won their share of titles over the course of their 100-plus year history. But after the events of 2003, the Tigers found themselves saddled with an unwanted new reputation: losers.

Managed and coached by popular members of the 1984 World Series champion Tigers (Alan Trammell and Kirk Gibson), the 2003 Tigers were outscored by 337 runs and finished 43–119, 47 games behind the Minnesota Twins in the AL Central. Were it not for a streak of 5 wins in 6 games to end the season, the Tigers would have shattered the 1962 New York Mets' record for losses in a single season.

The Tigers shed that "losers" tag as quickly as they'd acquired it. The team rebounded from a 119-loss season in 2003 to win 95 games in 2006 and represented the American League in the World Series that year.

> **The Tigers rebounded from a 119-loss season in 2003 to win 95 games in 2006.**

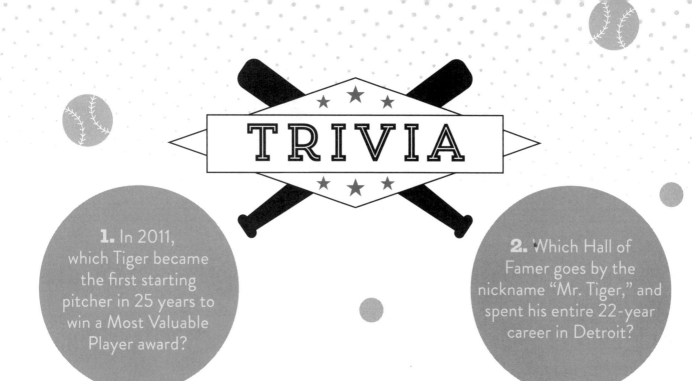

TRIVIA

1. In 2011, which Tiger became the first starting pitcher in 25 years to win a Most Valuable Player award?

2. Which Hall of Famer goes by the nickname "Mr. Tiger," and spent his entire 22-year career in Detroit?

THE TRIPLE CROWN

In 2012, Tigers third baseman Miguel Cabrera became the first player since 1967 to win the Triple Crown. He led the American League in 3 key offensive categories—batting average (.330), home runs (44) and runs batted in (139). Cabrera also ranked high in 2 other offensive categories that are arguably more important. He finished first in slugging percentage (.606) and fourth in on-base percentage (.393). Here's the short list of Triple Crown winners in baseball history:

Miguel Cabrera
(2012, American League)

Carl Yastrzemski
(1967, AL)

Frank Robinson
(1966, AL)

Mickey Mantle
(1956, AL)

Ted Williams
(1947, AL)

Ted Williams
(1942, AL)

Joe Medwick
(1937, National League)

Lou Gehrig
(1934, AL)

Jimmie Foxx
(1933, AL)

Chuck Klein
(1933, NL)

Rogers Hornsby
(1925, NL)

Rogers Hornsby
(1922, NL)

Ty Cobb
(1909, AL)

Nap Lajoie
(1901, AL)

Hugh Duffy
(1894, NL)

Tip O'Neill
(1887, American Association)

Paul Hines
(1878, NL)

KANSAS CITY ROYALS
★ GLORY DAYS ★

Few teams are remembered as fondly by their fans as the Kansas City Royals of the 1970s. Under the leadership of Hall of Fame manager Whitey Herzog, the Royals developed one of the era's strongest cores of talent, including pitcher Paul Splittorff, second baseman Frank White, outfielder Willie Wilson, and third baseman (and Hall of Famer) George Brett. The team won at least 85 games in every season between 1975 and 1980 and more than 90 games 5 times.

The Royals reached only 1 World Series during that stretch. In 1980, under new manager Jim Frey, they lost to the Philadelphia Phillies. But that era is remembered as fondly as the one that came next . . . which happened to feature the Royals' only World Series title (in 1985, over cross-state rivals the St. Louis Cardinals).

★ **The Royals won at least 85 games in every season between 1975 and 1980.**

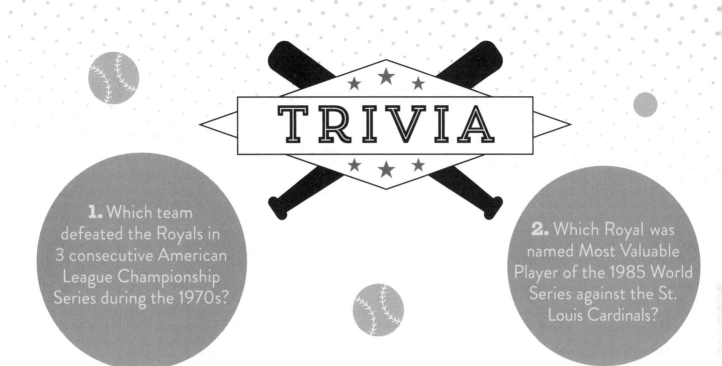

1. Which team defeated the Royals in 3 consecutive American League Championship Series during the 1970s?

2. Which Royal was named Most Valuable Player of the 1985 World Series against the St. Louis Cardinals?

THE LANGUAGE OF BASEBALL

Baseball has a vocabulary of its own:

Hot corner:
third base

Chin music:
a pitch thrown high and inside

Tattoo:
to hit the ball very hard

Wheels:
a speedy player ("that kid's got some wheels")

Captain Hook:
a manager who "hooks" (removes) his pitcher from the game at the earliest sign of trouble

Rope:
a strong throw, usually from an outfielder to either third base or home plate

Gopher ball:
a poorly placed pitch swatted for a home run

Can of corn:
an easily caught fly ball

Bandbox:
a small ballpark

Plunked:
hit by a pitch

Tater:
a home run

Going yard:
hitting a tater

Texas leaguer:
a weakly hit ball that drops between the infielders and the outfielders for a hit

Baltimore chop:
a ball hit hard into the ground in front of home plate that then bounces high enough to allow the batter to reach base

CLEVELAND INDIANS

★ CURSES? ★

For all the talk about cursed teams, the Indians are one of the few franchises that seem truly snakebitten. After winning the 1948 World Series, the talented Indians of the 1950s had the bad luck to be pitted against the even more talented New York Yankees of that decade. Cleveland's one 1950s pennant-winning team, in 1954, won 111 regular-season games but were upset in the World Series by the New York Giants.

The Indians spent most of the next 3 decades in or near last place in the American League before rising again in the mid-1990s—when they ran into another Yankees dynasty as well as talented teams from Boston and Baltimore. During one of their World Series appearances, in 1997, the Indians weren't able to hold a ninth-inning lead in the pivotal Game 7. Five playoff appearances since then haven't eased the sting, nor made the team's fans feel any less cursed.

TRIVIA

1. How many consecutive Gold Gloves did Omar Vizquel win upon joining the Indians prior to the 1994 season?

2. How many consecutive AL Central titles did the Indians win during the 1990s?

ROSTER RULES

On a basic level, there are 25 active players on a Major League roster. But as you'll see, it's not quite as simple as that.

> The 25-man roster expands to 26 for scheduled day-night doubleheaders, which is when 2 teams play an early afternoon and a night game on the same day . . . but only when the double header is scheduled 48 hours in advance.

> There's a 40-man roster as well, comprising of all the players who are signed to a Major League contract. Players on the 15-day disabled list are considered to be on the 40-man roster, but players on the 60-day disabled list and suspended players are not.

> In September the 25-man roster expands to 40. Any player on the 40-man roster is eligible to play.

> For the playoffs, active rosters consist of 25 players. No roster moves are allowed unless a player is moved to the disabled list.

CHICAGO WHITE SOX
★ THE OTHER TEAM IN TOWN? ★

The Chicago White Sox, like the New York Mets, have had the bad fortune of sharing a city with one of the game's most popular teams. But unlike the Mets, who won a World Series in their eighth season, it took a while for the White Sox to get on track.

The White Sox won a title in 1917 and returned to the World Series 2 years later. After that came a drought almost as long as the one Chicago Cubs fans have experienced. Despite a trip to the World Series in 1959, the Sox were at 88 title-less years and counting before they swept the Houston Astros in the 2005 World Series. They may still trail the Cubs in attendance, but the White Sox currently own on-field bragging rights.

★ **The White Sox won a title in 1917 and returned to the World Series 2 years later.**

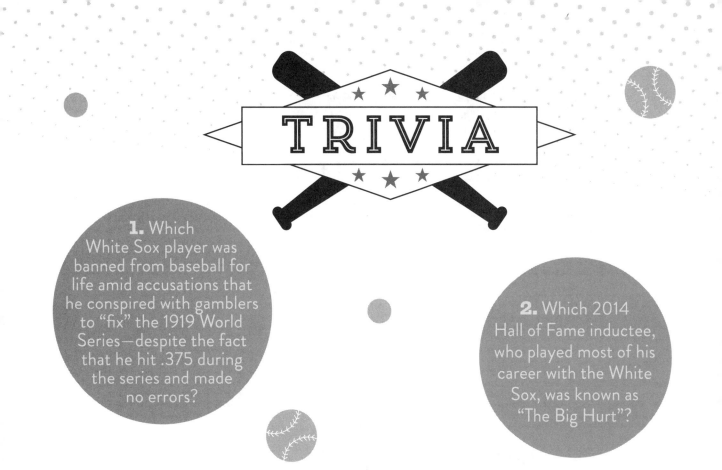

TRIVIA

1. Which White Sox player was banned from baseball for life amid accusations that he conspired with gamblers to "fix" the 1919 World Series—despite the fact that he hit .375 during the series and made no errors?

2. Which 2014 Hall of Fame inductee, who played most of his career with the White Sox, was known as "The Big Hurt"?

TRADITIONS & CEREMONIES

During his time owning the White Sox, Bill Veeck was as much a promoter as he was an owner. He outfitted the team in shorts, shot off fireworks whenever the Sox hit a home run, and held a Disco Demolition Night that ended in a riot (and the White Sox forfeiting the game). He's also credited with starting the tradition of singing "Take Me Out to the Ball Game" during the seventh-inning stretch, which is just one of many traditions and ceremonies that baseball works into the flow of the game.

Singing the national anthem before the start of the game

This practice, which was adopted by just about every other North American professional sports league, dates back to World War II.

Calling on a dignitary to throw out a ceremonial first pitch

William Taft was the first president to throw a first pitch, and nearly every president since then has done so at least once. Originally the pitch was thrown from the front row of the stands, but now the honoree goes into his or her windup from in front of the pitcher's mound.

Retiring numbers

Teams often remove from circulation the jersey numbers of their best or longest-tenured players. The first player to have his number (4) retired was the Yankees' Lou Gehrig. Major League Baseball retired Jackie Robinson's number (42) league-wide in 1997, allowing only players who were already wearing it to continue to do so.

MINNESOTA TWINS
★ IT'S ALL ABOUT TIMING ★

The former Washington Senators arrived in Minnesota in 1961, bringing with them the low expectations that come with any relocated franchise. As luck would have it, Minnesota got the Senators at precisely the right moment. Hall of Famer Harmon Killebrew was about to come into his own as a power hitter—he hit 46 home runs during his first season as a Twin—and he was joined by fellow future Hall of Famer Jim Kaat to form the core of a team that won the American League pennant in 1965.

A similar core of talent came together for the Twins in the mid-1980s, when Kirby Puckett, Kent Hrbek, and others hit their primes at nearly the same time. The result? World Series titles in both 1987 and 1991. Despite dominating the AL Central in the 2000s, the Twins haven't been back to the World Series since then.

TRIVIA

1. Which 2 teams did the Twins defeat to win their modern-era World Series titles?

2. In how many consecutive All-Star Games did Hall of Famer Rod Carew play?

THE PITCHES

The Twins' recent struggles can be traced in part to their pitching—in particular, their inability to develop young starters and keep them healthy. On any successful staff, pitchers will throw a wide variety of pitches, including but not limited to:

Fastball
Relies mostly on speed to avoid being hit

Cutter
A fastball thrown with a grip designed to create more spin

Split-Finger Fastball
A fastball thrown with a tight grip so that the ball dives as it approaches home plate

Curveball
Gripped with 3 fingers and thrown with a motion that causes it to "bend"

Slider
Gripped like a curveball but thrown with a downward motion that causes it to appear to move sideways

Knuckleball
Held loosely and released in a way that makes its motion unpredictable—even to the person throwing it

Changeup
Thrown with the same arm motion as a fastball, but it comes out of the pitcher's hand more slowly becuse of the grip

I was always glad I never had to face my teammate Mo's cut fastball.

AL CENTRAL POP QUIZ

Now that you've aced the AL CENTRAL, let's test your smarts! Score a single for 1 correct answer, a double for 2, and a triple for 3. How many runs can you score by the end of the book?

1. Which team did the Kansas City Royals defeat to win their only World Series title?

2. How many games did the 2003 Detroit Tigers lose?

3. In what year did the Cleveland Indians last win the World Series?

THEY SAID IT

Baseball as a sport has attracted some extremely smart and well-spoken athletes. It has also attracted some of the sports world's most creative users of the English language. Here's a compilation of some of the funniest, wisest, strangest, and most memorable baseball quotes, from individuals in and around the game:

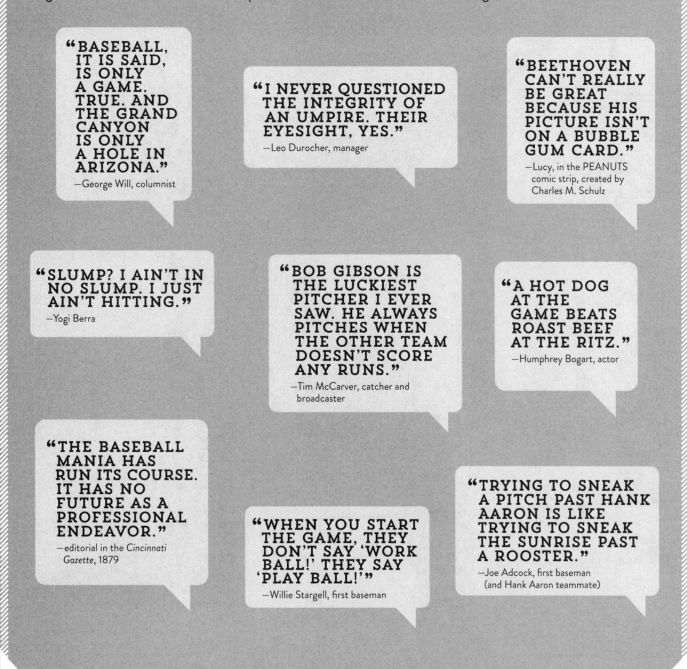

"BASEBALL, IT IS SAID, IS ONLY A GAME. TRUE. AND THE GRAND CANYON IS ONLY A HOLE IN ARIZONA."
—George Will, columnist

"I NEVER QUESTIONED THE INTEGRITY OF AN UMPIRE. THEIR EYESIGHT, YES."
—Leo Durocher, manager

"BEETHOVEN CAN'T REALLY BE GREAT BECAUSE HIS PICTURE ISN'T ON A BUBBLE GUM CARD."
—Lucy, in the PEANUTS comic strip, created by Charles M. Schulz

"SLUMP? I AIN'T IN NO SLUMP. I JUST AIN'T HITTING."
—Yogi Berra

"BOB GIBSON IS THE LUCKIEST PITCHER I EVER SAW. HE ALWAYS PITCHES WHEN THE OTHER TEAM DOESN'T SCORE ANY RUNS."
—Tim McCarver, catcher and broadcaster

"A HOT DOG AT THE GAME BEATS ROAST BEEF AT THE RITZ."
—Humphrey Bogart, actor

"THE BASEBALL MANIA HAS RUN ITS COURSE. IT HAS NO FUTURE AS A PROFESSIONAL ENDEAVOR."
—editorial in the *Cincinnati Gazette*, 1879

"WHEN YOU START THE GAME, THEY DON'T SAY 'WORK BALL!' THEY SAY 'PLAY BALL!'"
—Willie Stargell, first baseman

"TRYING TO SNEAK A PITCH PAST HANK AARON IS LIKE TRYING TO SNEAK THE SUNRISE PAST A ROOSTER."
—Joe Adcock, first baseman (and Hank Aaron teammate)

2014 RESULTS

Los Angeles Angels	98–64
Oakland Athletics	88–74
Seattle Mariners	87–75
Houston Astros	70–92
Texas Rangers	67–95

LOS ANGELES ANGELS OF ANAHEIM
★ CONFUSED? SO ARE WE. ★

The Angels franchise was founded in 1961 as the Los Angeles Angels and played its home games in Los Angeles until its own home park was ready. That park, however, was built in Anaheim, California, 25 miles outside Los Angeles—so the Angels changed their name, for the first time, to the California Angels. They became the second Major League team named after a state rather than a city; the Minnesota Twins were first.

That name didn't last. In 1996 the team became the Anaheim Angels. But following another ownership change, the Angels went back to a prior name, sort of. Since 2005 the team has been known as the Los Angeles Angels of Anaheim.

They Angels became the second **Major League** team named after a state rather than a city.

TRIVIA

1. Which current Angels player smacked more than 200 extra-base hits, stole more than 90 bases, and drove in more than 270 runs—before his 23rd birthday?

2. What Angels rookie pitcher won 5 games during the 2002 postseason, despite never having won a game during the regular season?

THE AWARDS

After the 2012 season, fans spent hours debating the selection of the Detroit Tigers' Miguel Cabrera as the American League Most Valuable Player over the Angels' Mike Trout. That's part of the fun of baseball's postseason honors, which are awarded following the conclusion of the World Series. Several are voted on by the Baseball Writers' Association of America, while others are decided by the managers or the Major League Baseball's commissioner's office.

Most Valuable Player
Given to the best all-around player (baseball allows voters to decide for themselves what constitutes "best all-around").

Cy Young
Given to the best pitcher, whether a starter or a reliever.

Rookie of the Year
Given to the best player who qualifies as a rookie (defined as having fewer than 130 at-bats, 50 innings pitched, or 45 days spent active on a Major League roster in any previous season).

Manager of the Year
Given to the manager who, at least in the minds of the voters, did the best job. Only once has the manager of a team with a losing record won this award (Joe Girardi, who managed the fourth-place 2006 Florida Marlins).

Gold Gloves
Given to the players who—again, at least in the minds of the selectors—fielded their positions most ably.

OAKLAND ATHLETICS
★ HOW ABOUT SOME RESPECT? ★

For a team that has won consistently over the years, the Oakland Athletics are rarely mentioned as one of the game's powerhouse franchises. The team has won 16 AL West titles and 2 Wild Card berths since joining the division in 1969. It won 3 straight World Series in the 1970s and reached 3 straight World Series, and won 1, between 1988 and 1990. It won 20 straight games in 2002.

The point is a simple one. Any list of baseball's best teams should include the Oakland A's.

TRIVIA

1. Who were the 3 A's who won the Rookie of the Year awards consecutively from 1986 to 1988?

2. What is the name of the book and the movie that documented how the A's have, during the last 2 decades, used innovative strategies to assemble and run a team?

THE UNWRITTEN RULES

Oakland has won 16 AL West titles and 2 Wild Card berths since 1969.

A few years ago when Alex Rodriguez of the New York Yankees walked across the pitcher's mound on his way back to the dugout, he found himself on the receiving end of a rant from Oakland pitcher Dallas Braden. By stepping on the mound, the Yankees player violated one of baseball's numerous "unwritten rules," ones monitored and enforced by the players themselves. Here are a few more:

For Base Runners
No stealing bases when the team has a large lead, no sliding with your spikes high

For Hitters
No bunting to break up a no-hitter; no excessive admiring of your own home runs

For Pitchers
Don't "show up" fielders who make an error behind you (that is, you shouldn't yell or pound your glove); do retaliate for a teammate who was intentionally hit by a pitch, by intentionally hitting an opposing batter (but always below the head)

I Remember being taught at an early age to put my head down and Run around the bases after a home Run.

SEATTLE MARINERS

★ THE BEST TEAM WITHOUT A TITLE? ★

Heading into the 2001 playoffs, the Seattle Mariners appeared to be on a mission. While they had tasted some playoff success a few years earlier, the Mariners headed into the postseason looking unbeatable. During the regular season they'd won 116 games—tying a Major League record—and had led the Majors in both runs scored and fewest opposing runs allowed. The roster was packed with in-their-prime hitters, including Edgar Martinez and Ichiro Suzuki.

And then, in a great example of the random nature of playoff baseball, the Mariners hit a wall. They lost to the New York Yankees, a team that had won 21 fewer regular-season games, in a quick American League Championship Series. The Mariners haven't returned to the playoffs since and until 2014 hadn't notched a winning record since 2009.

During the 2001 regular season, the Mariners won 116 games, tying a Major League record for the most wins in a season.

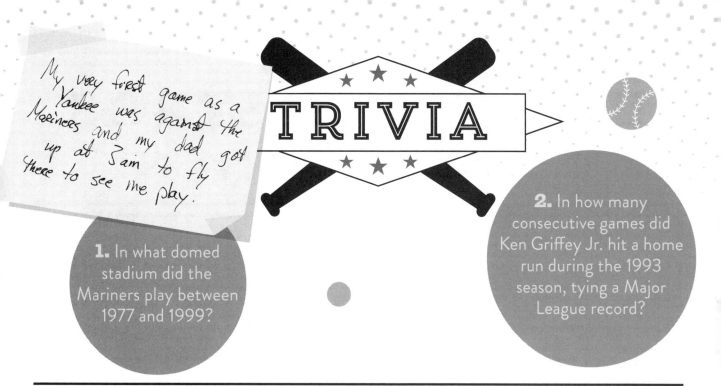

My very first game as a Yankee was against the Mariners and my dad got up at 3am to fly up there to see me play.

TRIVIA

1. In what domed stadium did the Mariners play between 1977 and 1999?

2. In how many consecutive games did Ken Griffey Jr. hit a home run during the 1993 season, tying a Major League record?

THE GEAR

Sometimes it seems like baseball players love accessories as much as models do. Here's a partial list of the gear that you might see on or around your favorite players:

Ball

It has a cork center that is surrounded by yarn and covered by leather, which is held together with 108 stitches. The official Major League ball weighs about 5 ounces.

Bat

In pro baseball, only bats made from a single piece of solid wood are legal. The wood most commonly used for a bat is ash, but sugar maple and hickory are sometimes used as well. Bats cannot be more than 2.75 inches in diameter or more than 42 inches long.

Gloves/Mitts

They've become more specialized over the years. A catcher's mitt has extra padding but no individual fingers. A first baseman's mitt is longer and wider (to help the user field errant throws and hops) and also lacks individual fingers. Infielders' gloves are small and have shallow pockets (to help their users transfer the ball from mitt to hand), while outfielders' gloves are long and deep-pocketed (to give their users a little extra reach).

Batting Gloves

Worn on one or both hands by batters, they're designed to protect the hands and absorb the shock that radiates down the bat when it makes contact with a pitched ball.

Catcher's Helmet

This is a helmet with a mask that protects the face. Until recently the catcher wore a mask over a batter's helmet. Newer catchers' helmets resemble hockey goalie masks.

HOUSTON ASTROS

★ TRADING SPACES ★

In 2013, the Astros became the first franchise to switch leagues in 15 years. The Astros moved from the NL Central to the AL West, which made the number of teams in each league 15 and the number of teams in each division 5.

The move had a major effect on the schedule. With an odd number of teams in each league, it was necessary for baseball to schedule interleague games (American League team versus National League team) throughout the season—and starting in 2013, interleague games were played just about every day of the season. Since its introduction in 1997, interleague play had mostly taken place during the months of May and June, and usually prior to the All-Star Break.

TRIVIA

1. Which Hall of Fame pitcher logged 1,866 of his MLB-record 5,714 strikouts as a member of the Astros?

2. What 2 players formed the core of the "Killer B's" Astros that made the playoffs 6 times in 9 seasons between 1997 and 2005?

(1. Nolan Ryan)

(2. Jeff Bagwell and Craig Biggio)

THE GOOD, THE BAD, THE UGLY, AND THE REALLY UGLY

It's hard to win more than 100 games in a season. It might be harder to lose more than 100 games, as the Astros did in 2011, 2012, and 2013. Here are baseball's 5 best and 5 worst regular-season records:

Best

1906 Chicago Cubs (116–36, .763 winning percentage)

1902 Pittsburgh Pirates (103–36, .741)

1886 Chicago White Stockings (90–34, .726)

1909 Pittsburgh Pirates (110–42, .724)

1954 Cleveland Indians (111–43, .721)

Worst

1899 Cleveland Spiders (20–134, .130 winning percentage)

1890 Pittsburgh Pirates (23–113, .169)

1916 Philadelphia Athletics (36–117, .235)

1935 Boston Braves (38–115, .248)

1962 New York Mets (40–120, .250)

In 2013, the Astros became the first franchise to switch leagues in 15 years.

TEXAS RANGERS

★ THE NEW TEAM IN TOWN ★

Texas has always been considered a football-first state, with even high school football games generating huge attendance and media interest. So the Rangers had an uphill battle when they arrived in Arlington, Texas, in time for the 1972 season, and that was before you factored in the summer heat and humidity.

Despite a 94-win season in 1977 and a second-place AL West finish in both 1977 and 1986, the Rangers didn't truly win over fans until . . . well, until they started winning regularly. In the second half of the 1990s an offense-first team featuring Ivan Rodriguez, Juan Gonzalez, and Rusty Greer won 3 AL West titles in 4 years. Playoff success didn't come until more than a decade later, when the Rangers won consecutive American League titles and came within 1 out of winning the 2011 World Series.

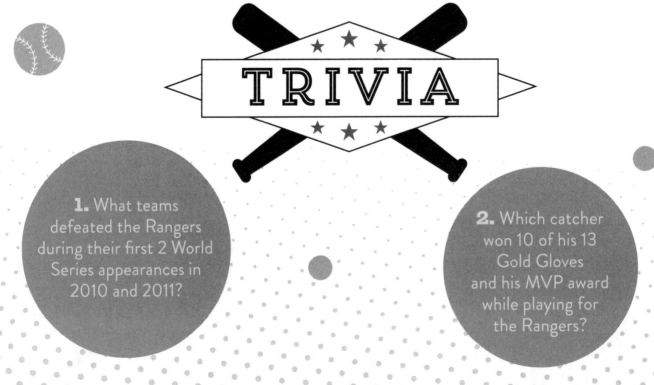

TRIVIA

1. What teams defeated the Rangers during their first 2 World Series appearances in 2010 and 2011?

2. Which catcher won 10 of his 13 Gold Gloves and his MVP award while playing for the Rangers?

THE MEN IN BLUE

As hard as it is to imagine, a single umpire used to officiate games by himself during baseball's early years. That changed as baseball became more complicated during the early 1900s, and now regular-season games are umpired by a 4-man crew.

Home Plate Umpire

Calls balls and strikes and makes most calls near home plate. If a base umpire ventures into the outfield to cover a play, the home plate umpire may move to cover the unattended base.

Base Umpires

Stationed near first, second, and third base. The first base and third base umpires are often called on to decide whether a batter has checked his swing.

Outfield Umpires

For the All-Star Game and the playoffs, baseball adds 2 more umpires—1 along the left-field line and 1 along the right-field line.

The Rangers didn't truly win over fans until they started winning regularly.

AL WEST POP QUIZ

Now that you've aced the AL WEST, let's test your smarts! Score a single for 1 correct answer, a double for 2, and a triple for 3. How many runs can you score by the end of the book?

> **1.** How many consecutive regular-season games did the Oakland A's win during their 2002 streak?

> **2.** What are the 4 names by which the Angels franchise has been known since 1961?

> **3.** In what season did the Seattle Mariners last qualify for the playoffs?

LIGHTS, CAMERA, ACTION:
THE BEST BASEBALL MOVIES FOR KIDS

THE SANDLOT (1993)
A new kid moves to town and has a tough time making friends—that is, until he falls in with a group of kids who play baseball every day at a small neighborhood field.

LITTLE BIG LEAGUE (1994)
When he becomes the owner (and eventually the manager) of the Minnesota Twins, a young boy gets to live out the dream of not-so-young boys everywhere.

EVERYONE'S HERO (ANIMATED, 2006)
A young fan attempts to help his father, who works as a janitor at Yankee Stadium, after he is accused of stealing Babe Ruth's famous bat.

THE ROOKIE (2002)
A former pitching prospect makes his way back to the Major Leagues after quitting the game in the wake of a shoulder injury. The movie is based on the true story of Rays pitcher Jim Morris.

THE BAD NEWS BEARS (1976)
A cranky former minor-league pitcher takes a motley crew of players under his wing and coaches them toward the playoffs.

ROOKIE OF THE YEAR (1993)
After his broken arm heals, a 12-year-old discovers that he can throw the ball as well as any professional pitcher and goes to play for the Chicago Cubs.

ANGELS IN THE OUTFIELD (1994)
A young child prays for somebody to help his terrible California Angels win games—and a group of angels answers the prayer, helping the team win in unexpected ways.

WHAT IS YOUR FAVORITE BASEBALL MOVIE?

My favorite baseball movie is "Major League."

EAST

NATIONAL LEAGUE

2014 RESULTS

Washington Nationals	96–66
Atlanta Braves	79–83
New York Mets	79–83
Miami Marlins	77–85
Philadelphia Phillies	73–89

WASHINGTON NATIONALS

★ THIRD TIME'S A CHARM ★

Baseball has a long and storied history in the city of Washington, DC, with the earliest known teams dating back to 1871. The current Washington Nationals claimed back some of that history, as several of those teams also used the Nationals name.

The first Washington Senators (known as the Nationals for a stretch) played in the American League from 1901 to 1960, after which they moved to Minnesota and renamed themselves the Twins. The second Washington Senators were an expansion team that played in the American League from 1961 to 1971, when they departed for Texas and became the Rangers. Meanwhile, this current version of the Washington, DC, franchise formerly called Montreal its home.

TRIVIA

1. Which Nationals pitcher struck out 92 batters over 68 innings in his first 12 big-league starts, before an arm injury sidelined him the rest of his rookie season?

2. Which former top MLB draft pick won NL Rookie of the Year as a 19-year-old, following a season in which he hit 22 home runs and stole 18 bases?

(1. Stephen Strasburg)

(2. Bryce Harper)

ON THE MOVE

Just as Washington, DC, lost 2 teams, so too did another city have to lose its team in order for baseball to return to Washington. That team was the Montreal Expos, an NL East institution from their founding in 1969 until their departure following the 2004 season. Here are a few facts about the much-missed Expos:

➤ Won a single NL East title, in 1981

➤ Had baseball's best record, 74–40, when a players' strike led to the cancellation of the rest of the 1994 season

➤ As of July 2014, 5 Hall of Famers played for or managed the Expos for at least part of their careers: Gary Carter, Andre Dawson, Tony Perez, Frank Robinson, and Dick Williams

➤ Pitchers threw 4 no-hitters during the Expos' brief life, the first of which came in the team's ninth game

➤ During their final 3 seasons, the Expos were owned by Major League Baseball

➤ During the 2003 and 2004 seasons, the Expos played some of their "home" games in San Juan, Puerto Rico

The earliest known team in Washington dates back to 1871.

ATLANTA BRAVES

★A DECADE (AND THEN SOME) OF DOMINANCE★

For much of the 1970s and 1980s, the Braves were one of baseball's worst teams. That all changed in 1991, when the worst-to-first Braves outlasted the Los Angeles Dodgers to win the NL West by a single game. This began a run during which the Braves won their division—first the NL West and then the NL East—14 consecutive times.

During this stretch the Braves advanced to the World Series 5 times between 1991 and 1999, and won it once, in 1995. Whether or not the Braves won as many championship titles as their fans would have liked, it's unlikely that baseball will see this kind of division dominance again anytime soon.

TRIVIA

1. Which Braves legend became the all-time home-run leader—a record he'd hold for more than 33 years—when he connected for home run number 715 on April 8, 1974?

2. What team broke the Braves' streak of 11 straight NL East titles in 2006?

THE NAME GAME, PART ONE

Thanks to broadcasts of their games on the TBS cable network, the Braves of the 1980s and beyond generated a large fan base outside Atlanta. This exposure landed the team the designation of "America's Team," and the trio of Greg Maddux, Tom Glavine, and John Smoltz the nickname "The Big Three." Here are some other names that have captured fans' imagination in recent years:

The Killer B's

During the 1990s and 2000s, the Houston Astros happened to have a large contingent of players with last names that started with *B*. The core of the Killer B's during this era were Craig Biggio, Jeff Bagwell, and Lance Berkman, though several other players (Derek Bell, Carlos Beltran, and Sean Berry among them) were part of the Killer B's for a season or 2.

The Nasty Boys

The highest compliment one can give to a pitch is to call it "nasty." In 1990 the Cincinnati Reds had 3 relief pitchers whose offerings qualified—Norm Charlton, Rob Dibble, and Randy Myers, who became known as the Nasty Boys. Collectively they notched 44 saves that season and helped the Reds win the 1990 World Series.

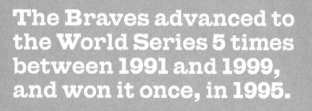

I love being a member of what people call the "Core Four" with Pettitte, Rivera, and Posada. We all made our Yankee MLB debuts in 1995.

The Braves advanced to the World Series 5 times between 1991 and 1999, and won it once, in 1995.

NEW YORK METS

★ OCCASIONALLY AMAZIN' ★

Technically the Mets weren't the second team in New York: They were the fourth during baseball's modern era, following the Yankees, Brooklyn Dodgers, and New York Giants. After the Dodgers and Giants relocated to California, the Mets arrived as an expansion team in 1962—and introduced themselves with one of the worst campaigns in baseball history, finishing 40–120.

While the Mets may have existed in the Yankees' shadow for much of their history, they've experienced plenty of glory of their own. Though the team had previously never finished higher than second-to-last in the National League, the 1969 "Miracle Mets" beat the Baltimore Orioles to win the World Series in what's still considered one of the game's biggest upsets. In 1986 a Mets team down to its last out in Game 6 rallied to win a 7-game classic World Series over the Boston Red Sox. The Yankees don't hold an exclusive claim on New York baseball glory.

TRIVIA

1. In what way did the Mets honor the Brooklyn Dodgers and the New York Giants, the 2 teams that had previously called New York home?

2. Of the 12 Baseball Hall-of-Famers who played for the Mets at some point in their career, who is the only one depicted wearing a Mets cap on his Hall of Fame plaque?

(1. the Mets adopted their uniform colors, combining Dodgers blue with Giants orange)

(2. Tom Seaver)

STARS SHINING BRIGHTLY

The Major League Baseball All-Star Game, which the Mets hosted during the 2013 season, was first played in 1933. Other facts about the All-Star Game include:

> The first MLB All-Star Game was held as part of the 1933 World's Fair in Chicago (at Comiskey Park) and was intended as a one-time-only exhibition.

> From 1959 to 1962, 2 All-Star Games were held each season.

> Starting in 1962, baseball named an All-Star Game Most Valuable Player.

> The 2002 All-Star Game was declared a tie because both teams ran out of available pitchers.

Fans were not happy after 11 innings when Commissioner Bud Selig declared it a 7-7 tie.

> The only MLB franchises that have not hosted an All-Star Game are the Tampa Bay Rays and the Miami Marlins.

> The AL and NL teams are managed by the managers of the teams that played in the previous season's World Series.

> The players are selected by a combination of fan voting, player voting, and manager decision, with the league office designating replacements if needed.

> Since 2003 the league that wins the All-Star Game has been awarded home-field advantage for the World Series.

MIAMI MARLINS
★ UPS AND DOWNS ★

The Marlins' brief history is unlike any other team's. In their 22 seasons—the first 19 as the Florida Marlins—they qualified for the playoffs 2 times.

Both times they won the World Series. And after each win, because of trades that rid the team of its most expensive players, the Marlins quickly fell back toward mediocrity.

After winning the 1997 World Series, the 1998 Marlins went 54–108. The teams that followed the 2003 World Series champions fared better, finishing 83–79 in both 2004 and 2005, but the Marlins haven't experienced much success since then. In 13 of its 22 seasons, the team has finished either last or next to last in its division.

After winning the 1997 World Series, the 1998 Marlins went 54-108. ★

TRIVIA

1. The Marlins' new ballpark, which opened for the start of the 2012 season, was built on the site of what former stadium?

2. Which 23-year-old pitcher threw a 5-hit shutout in Game 6 of the 2003 World Series and was ultimately named Series MVP?

IT'S ALL ABOUT OCTOBER

Baseball's playoffs have evolved to include more teams and more rounds over the years.

Prior to 1969

Only 2 teams qualified for the playoffs, which pitted the winner of the National League against the winner of the American League in the best-of-7 World Series. (In 1903, 1919, 1920, and 1921 the World Series was best-of-9.)

1969 to 1993

After both 12-team leagues were split into Eastern and Western divisions, baseball expanded its playoffs to 2 rounds. The winners of the East and West faced off in the best-of-5 League Championship Series, with the survivors moving on to face each other in the World Series. In 1985 the League Championship Series was expanded to a best-of-7 format.

1994 to 2011

The American and National Leagues were each split into 3 divisions. Those 6 division winners were joined in the playoffs by a Wild Card from each league, the team with the best record that hadn't won its division. The playoffs then became a 3-round affair: the so-called Division Series (best of 5), League Championship Series (best of 7), and World Series (best of 7).

2012 to Present

Baseball added a second Wild Card to the playoffs and, in each league, pitted the 2 Wild Cards in a single-elimination game to see who advanced to the Division Series.

(1. the Orange Bowl, which hosted one of college football's most famous postseason bowl games prior to its demolition in 2008)

(2. Josh Beckett)

PHILADELPHIA PHILLIES

★ LOTS OF *L*s ★

The Phillies are as much of an institution as any other team in any sport. Founded in 1883, they are the oldest franchise in American professional sports to play, without interruption, in a single city under a single name.

Of course, anyone who has been around that long has likely experienced many ups and downs. In July of 2007 the Phillies became the first team in MLB history to lose 10,000 games. Their fans didn't seem to mind, especially since the team qualified for the playoffs that season and did so again every season through 2011.

★ Founded in **1883**, the Phillies are one of the oldest franchises in American professional sports.

TRIVIA

1. Which Hall of Fame third baseman played his entire 18-year career with the Phillies, hitting 548 home runs and driving in 1,595 runs?

2. Which team was the first to join the Phillies in the 10,000-loss club?

THE
NAME GAME, PART TWO

For former center fielder and 8-time Gold Glove winner Garry "Secretary of Defense" Maddox, the Phillies coined one of the most memorable individual nicknames in baseball history. Of course, over the 100-plus years of organized baseball, some of the game's other best players have come to be known by colorful nicknames.

Mordecai "Three Finger" Brown

Shane "the Flyin' Hawaiian" Victorino

Gary "Kid" Carter

Ty "the Georgia Peach" Cobb

Willie "Pops" Stargell

Ted "Splendid Splinter" Williams

Phil "Scooter" Rizzuto

Babe "the Bambino" Ruth (also "the Sultan of Swat")

Honus "the Flying Dutchman" Wagner

Harmon "Killer" Killebrew

Stan "the Man" Musial

Reggie "Mr. October" Jackson

Willie "the Say Hey Kid" Mays

Dwight "Doc" Gooden

NL EAST POP QUIZ

Now that you've aced the NL EAST, let's test your smarts! Score a single for 1 correct answer, a double for 2, and a triple for 3. How many runs can you score by the end of the book?

1. What team was the first in baseball history to lose 10,000 games?

2. During the 1990s and 2000s, how many consecutive times did the Atlanta Braves win their division?

3. In what year did the New York Mets join the National League?

FANTASY FUN

Nobody knows for sure who first came up with the idea for fantasy sports—*On the Road* author Jack Kerouac is said to have played his own version of fantasy baseball in the 1930s—but the game began to grow in popularity during the 1980s. A group of journalists, led by editor and writer Daniel Okrent, started a league in 1980. They named it Rotisserie League Baseball, after the New York City restaurant in which many of the early drafts were conducted.

The rules for fantasy baseball have evolved, and websites allow players to customize the game to account for different levels of skill and involvement. Many leagues now allow "keepers," which means owners can keep players on their roster for longer than a single season. Most of the basic rules, however, remain just as they were during the game's first years.

owners draft players from
the list of active Major Leaguers

points are awarded based on the
real-life statistics of those players

hitting stat categories include batting average, home runs,
runs batted in, and stolen bases

pitching stat categories include wins, earned run average,
saves, and WHIP (walks + hits per inning pitched)

teams can be chosen through a player auction (highest bidder wins)
or through a draft (owners pick players 1 by 1 until rosters are filled)

a typical roster might include 25 players,
18 active (C, 1B, 2B, 3B, SS, OF, OF, OF,
utility, utility, SP, SP, RP, RP, P, P, P, P)
and 7 reserve

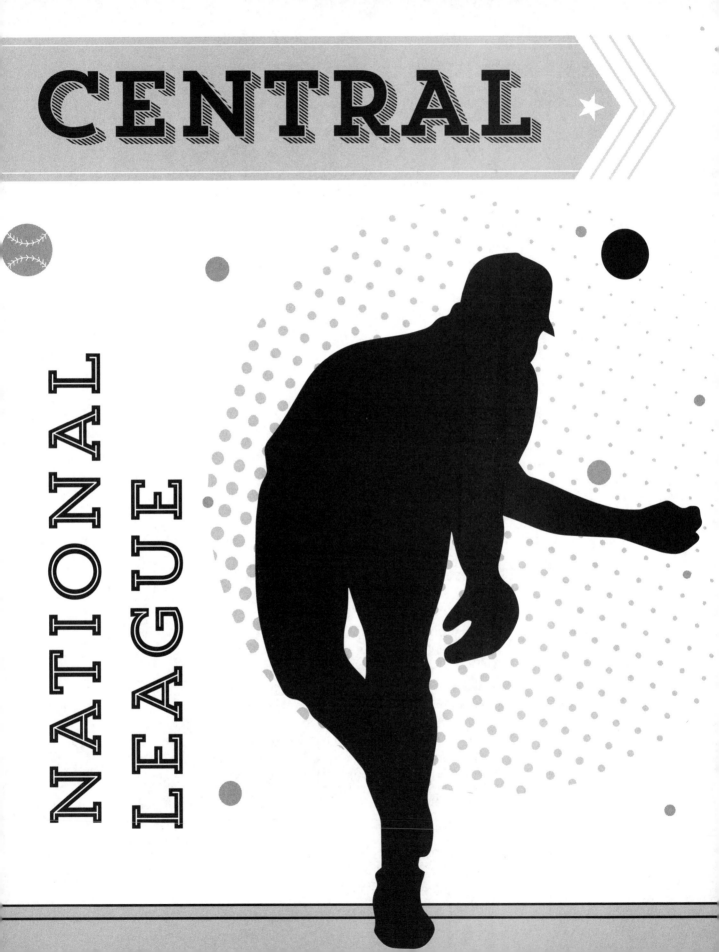

CENTRAL

NATIONAL LEAGUE

2014 RESULTS

St. Louis Cardinals	90–72
Pittsburgh Pirates	88–74
Milwaukee Brewers	82–80
Cincinnati Reds	76–86
Chicago Cubs	73–89

ST. LOUIS CARDINALS
★ SMALL MARKET, BIG SUCCESS ★

Compared with baseball host cities such as New York, Los Angeles, Chicago, and Houston, St. Louis is small. Despite that, the Cardinals have achieved more success—11 World Series titles and 19 National League championships—than almost anyone else.

Only the New York Yankees have won more World Series titles. The list of elite players who spent much of their career with the Cardinals, goes a long way toward explaining this. That list includes renowned executive Branch Rickey; manager Whitey Herzog; position players Stan Musial, Rogers Hornsby, Ozzie Smith, Albert Pujols, Yadier Molina, Red Schoendienst, and Joe Medwick; and pitchers Bob Gibson, Dizzy Dean, Chris Carpenter, Adam Wainwright, and Bruce Sutter.

The Cardinals have won 11 World Series titles and 19 NL Championships.

TRIVIA

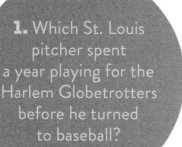

1. Which St. Louis pitcher spent a year playing for the Harlem Globetrotters before he turned to baseball?

2. Which Cardinals first baseman won 3 MVP awards and never hit fewer than 32 home runs or drove in fewer than 99 runs during his 11 years with the team?

THE 10,000 WIN CLUB

In 2009 the Cardinals became the fourth team to win its 10,000th game. Since then 3 other teams have achieved that same milestone. These are the game's great franchises, at least by the measure of wins:

San Francisco Giants 10,780

Chicago Cubs 10,511

Los Angeles Dodgers 10,489

St. Louis Cardinals 10,471

Atlanta Braves 10,303

Cincinnati Reds 10,257

Pittsburgh Pirates 10,143

PITTSBURGH PIRATES
★ FINALLY! ★

Compared with many other teams, the Pirates have a legacy of success. They won the World Series in 1960, 1971, and 1979, and advanced to 3 straight National League Championship Series between 1990 and 1992. Since that run of success, however, the team has fallen on hard times.

Prior to 2013, the Pirates posted a winning record exactly 0 times after the 1992 season. This was the longest un-winning streak in North American sports history. The team's fortunes finally turned in 2013, when it won more games than it lost, and claimed a Wild Card playoff berth. Given that many of the team's key players are young and are signed to long-term contracts, the Pirates' 2013 and 2014 performance could be a sign of things to come.

TRIVIA

1. Which player hit the walk-off home run that lifted the underdog Pirates to a win over the New York Yankees in Game 7 of the 1960 Word Series?

2. For how many consecutive seasons did slugger Ralph Kiner lead the National League in home runs?

THE SENIOR CIRCUIT

The National League was founded on February 2, 1876. William Hulbert, an executive with the Chicago White Stockings, had become frustrated with the existing league's lack of authority. After speaking with the owners of other teams, he unified them under the National League banner. While game play began immediately—on April 22, 1876—only a few of the league's 8 charter franchises survived to see the 1900s.

Chicago White Stockings
(now the Chicago Cubs)

New York Mutuals
(expelled after 1876)

Philadelphia Athletics
(expelled after 1876)

St. Louis Brown Stockings
(folded after 1877)

Boston Red Stockings
(now the Atlanta Braves)

Cincinnati Reds
(expelled after 1880)

Hartford Dark Blues
(folded after 1877)

Louisville Grays
(folded after 1877)

The Pirates have a legacy of success.

MILWAUKEE BREWERS
★ LOCAL HEROES ★

The city of Milwaukee has a long history of baseball, but not all of it was played by the Brewers. The city hosted an American League team for a single season in the early 1900s and a National League team for 13 seasons during the 1950s and 1960s.

The town's baseball champion was an unlikely candidate—Bud Selig, a local car salesman. He acquired the Seattle Pilots in 1970 and moved it to Milwaukee. He became Major League Baseball's acting commissioner in 1992 and his family sold the team to its current owner in 2005.

TRIVIA

1. In what year did the Milwaukee Brewers move from the American League to the National League?

2. What current teams besides the Brewers have never won a World Series?

(2. Tampa Bay Rays, Seattle Mariners, Houston Astros, Texas Rangers, Washington Nationals, San Diego Padres, and Colorado Rockies)

HIT KINGS

Paul Molitor, who played 15 of his 21 Major League seasons with the Brewers, ranks ninth on the career hits leaderboard. Here's the rest of the top 15, along with their hit totals:

1. Pete Rose (4,256 hits)

2. Ty Cobb (4,189)

3. Hank Aaron (3,771)

4. Stan Musial (3,630)

5. Tris Speaker (3,514)

6. Derek Jeter (3,465)

7. Cap Anson (3,435)

8. Honus Wagner (3,420)

9. Carl Yastrzemski (3,419)

10. Paul Molitor (3,319)

11. Eddie Collins (3,315)

12. Willie Mays (3,283)

13. Eddie Murray (3,255)

14. Nap Lajoie (3,243)

15. Cal Ripken Jr. (3,184)

This is a list I'm proud to be on.

CINCINNATI REDS

★ THE TEAM THAT BECAME A MACHINE ★

The Reds hold the title of baseball's oldest team. They were founded in 1869 as the Cincinnati Red Stockings and joined the National League for the first time in 1876. The team's name was shortened, according to rumor, so that it would fit more easily in newspaper headlines.

The Reds of the 1970s arguably hold another title—baseball's best team. "The Big Red Machine," as they were known, won 6 division titles and reached the World Series 4 times during the 1970s, and won in 1975 and 1976. The team's best players during this era included Pete Rose, Tony Perez, Johnny Bench, George Foster, Joe Morgan, and Ken Griffey Sr.

The Big Red Machine, won 6 division titles and reached the World Series 4 times during the 1970s.

TRIVIA

1. Which Reds first baseman notched a .424 on-base percentage and a .600 slugging percentage on his way to winning the 2010 National League MVP?

2. Sparky Anderson, who managed the Big Red Machine teams of the 1970s, became the first manager to accomplish what feat?

THE
NAME GAME, PART THREE

The Big Red Machine is one of baseball's most colorful team nicknames, but it's hardly the only one.

Harvey's Wallbangers

The 1982 Brewers could hit, and their manager's first name was Harvey. A nickname was thus born.

The Gashouse Gang

The 1934 St. Louis Cardinals often didn't wash their uniforms before taking the field, and their sloppy look and resulting smell reportedly gave rise to the "Gashouse Gang" tag.

The Amazin's

In their first 7 years of existence, the New York Mets never finished better than ninth in the 10-team National League. In 1969, following a slow start, they went 82–39 in their final 121 regular-season games and won the World Series.

Murderers' Row

The first 6 hitters in the 1927 Yankee lineup—Earle Combs, Mark Koenig, Babe Ruth, Lou Gehrig, Bob Meusel, and Tony Lazzeri—battered opposing pitchers. Finishing with a record of 110–44 and sweeping the Pittsburgh Pirates in the World Series, the '27 Yanks were perhaps baseball's most dominant offensive team.

(1. Joey Votto)

(2. To manage a winning World Series team in both leagues)

CHICAGO CUBS
★ THE WRONG KIND OF STREAK ★

The Cubs are one of the oldest teams in pro sports and have long drawn enthusiastic crowds to Wrigley Field. But they're known, unfortunately, for the wrong type of streak. Of all the teams in professional baseball—of all the teams in North American professional sports—the Cubs have gone the longest stretch since winning a championship. They last won the World Series in 1908 and extended their title drought to 106 seasons in 2014. The closest the Cubs have come was in 2003, when they were within 5 outs of defeating the Florida Marlins and advancing to their first World Series since 1945. But an error, a walk, and possible fan interference with a catchable foul ball led to a painful loss in that game. The Cubs then lost Game 7 of the League Championship Series the next night.

TRIVIA

1. Which 2014 Hall of Fame inductee and 355-game winner started his 23-season career with the Cubs?

2. Which Hall of Famer and member of the 500-home-run club was known as "Mr. Cub?"

(1. Greg Maddux)

(2. Ernie Banks)

OUCH!

The Cubs are not the only team that has experienced heartbreaking defeat in October.

In 1986, the Boston Red Sox were up 2 runs on the New York Mets in the bottom of the tenth inning of Game 6 of the World Series. They were 1 out away from winning their first World Series title since 1918. Then came 3 hits, a wild pitch, and an error, and a defeat that any Red Sox fan will tell you still stings.

In 2011 the Texas Rangers twice had a 2-run lead over the St. Louis Cardinals late in Game 6 of the World Series—once in the ninth inning and once in the tenth—and were twice within a single strike of winning the team's first championship. But a 2-run triple tied the game in the ninth inning, and a single tied the game again in the tenth. In the eleventh inning the Cardinals won the game on a solo home run. The next night they shut out the Rangers in Game 7 to win the World Series.

The Cubs last won the World Series in 1908. They came closest to winning again in 2003.

NL CENTRAL POP QUIZ

Now that you've aced the NL CENTRAL, let's test your smarts! Score a single for 1 correct answer, a double for 2, and a triple for 3. How many runs can you score by the end of the book?

1. What member of the NL Central holds the title of baseball's oldest team?

2. Prior to making the playoffs as a Wild Card in 2013, when was the last time the Pittsburgh Pirates qualified for postseason play?

3. In what year did the Chicago Cubs last win the World Series?

THE MASCOTS

If you attend a Yankees, Angels, or Dodgers home game, you might notice that something is missing—namely, a team mascot clad (more or less) in team colors and interacting with fans, players, and umpires alike. The first mascot, Mr. Met, made his (its?) debut when the Mets opened Shea Stadium in 1964. Since then he has been joined by quite a few furry friends. Some teams, in fact, have more than 1.

Ace and **Ace Jr.** (Toronto Blue Jays)
Bernie Brewer and **the Famous Racing Sausages** (Milwaukee Brewers)
Billy the Marlin (Miami Marlins)
Clark the Cub (Chicago Cubs)
D. Baxter the Bobcat and **the D-backs Luchador** (Arizona Diamondbacks)
Dinger (Colorado Rockies)
Fredbird and **Rally Squirrel** (St. Louis Cardinals)
Homer the Brave (Atlanta Braves)
Lou Seal (San Francisco Giants)
Mariner Moose (Seattle Mariners)
Mr. Met and **Mrs. Met** (New York Mets)
Mr. Red, Gapper, Rosie Red, and **Mr. Redlegs** (Cincinnati Reds)
Orbit (Houston Astros)
Oriole Bird (Baltimore Orioles)
Paws (Detroit Tigers)
Phillie Phanatic (Philadelphia Phillies)
Pirate Parrot, Captain Jolly Roger, and **The Pierogies** (Pittsburgh Pirates)
Rangers Captain (Texas Rangers)
Raymond and **DJ Kitty** (Tampa Bay Rays)
Screech and **the Presidents** (Washington Nationals)
Slider (Cleveland Indians)
Sluggerrr (Kansas City Royals)
Southpaw (Chicago White Sox)
Stomper (Oakland A's)
Swinging Friar (San Diego Padres)
T.C. Bear (Minnesota Twins)
Wally the Green Monster, Lefty, and **Righty** (Boston Red Sox)

WEST

NATIONAL LEAGUE

2014 RESULTS

Los Angeles Dodgers	94–68
San Francisco Giants	88–74
San Diego Padres	77–85
Colorado Rockies	66–96
Arizona Diamondbacks	64–98

LOS ANGELES DODGERS

★ HEARTBREAKERS ★

The Dodgers have won 5 World Series titles and packed Dodger Stadium since arriving in California in 1958. There are still millions of fans who will never forgive the team for abandoning Brooklyn, where it had played under several names since 1883.

While businessman and longtime Dodgers owner Walter O'Malley has been labeled a villain for moving the team across the country, politicians in the New York area share the blame. O'Malley wanted to build a new stadium in Brooklyn, but city planners refused to let him replace crumbling Ebbets Field. To this day, O'Malley is hated by Brooklyn fans.

I Remember my dad telling me stories about the Brooklyn Dodgers as a kid, and how mad the fans were when they moved to L.A.

The Dodgers famously started out in Brooklyn, where they first played in 1883. ★

TRIVIA

1. Which former Dodgers pitcher holds the record for the most consecutive scoreless innings thrown?

2. Which 2 Major League stadiums are older than Dodger Stadium?

MOVING RIGHT ALONG

The Dodgers are one of a number of teams that have relocated. The others include:

Washington Nationals (used to play in Montreal)

Atlanta Braves (Boston and Milwaukee)

San Francisco Giants (New York)

Milwaukee Brewers (Seattle)

Baltimore Orioles (Milwaukee and St. Louis)

Texas Rangers (Washington, DC)

Oakland Athletics (Philadelphia and Kansas City)

Minnesota Twins (Kansas City and Washington, DC)

(1. Orel Hershiser, who didn't allow a run in 59 innings during 1 month in 1988)

(2. Boston's Fenway Park and Chicago's Wrigley Field)

SAN FRANCISCO GIANTS

★ HALL PASS ★

The Giants have enjoyed tremendous success over the span of their long history, winning 8 World Series championships and 23 National League titles since their founding as the New York Gothams in 1883. It's no surprise, then, that more National Baseball Hall of Famers have at some point played for the Giants franchise than for any other team. Sixty-six onetime Giants—55 players and 11 managers—are currently enshrined, a total that outpaces the Los Angeles Dodgers (54) and New York Yankees (52).

The National Baseball Hall of Fame, located in Cooperstown, New York, was founded in 1936 and formally opened its doors in 1939. Players are elected into the Hall of Fame by both the Baseball Writers' Association of America and the Veterans Committee. Each year roughly 30 to 40 players are listed on the Hall of Fame ballot. Through July 2014, 306 individuals had been elected to the Hall of Fame: 246 former players; 22 managers; 10 umpires; and 28 executives, organizers, and "pioneers."

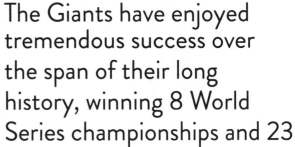

The Giants won the 2010, 2012, and 2014 World Series.

TRIVIA

1. Which longtime Giants player, known as the "Say Hey Kid," finished his career with 3,283 hits, 660 home runs, and 338 stolen bases?

2. What Giants player hit "the shot heard round the world," which still ranks among baseball's most memorable home runs?

THE IMMORTALS

The first Hall of Fame class, in 1936, included a mere 5 players:

Babe Ruth

Christy Mathewson

Walter Johnson

Ty Cobb

Honus Wagner

(1. Willie Mays)

(2. Bobby Thomson, in 1951. The home run was hit in the bottom of the ninth inning in the third game of a 3-game playoff to decide whether the Giants or the Brooklyn Dodgers would advance to the World Series.)

SAN DIEGO PADRES
★ NO NO-NOS ★

The Padres have celebrated many successes since they started playing in 1969—a pair of trips to the World Series and 5 NL West titles, among others. But after New York Mets pitcher Johan Santana threw a no-hitter in the franchise's 8,020th game, the Padres became the sole holder of a dubious record: They're the only 1 of baseball's 30 teams without a no-hitter to their name. Given that there have been 287 no-hitters in baseball history—and that long-gone organizations like the Louisville Colonels and the Hartford Dark Blues are among the teams with at least 1 of them—that's no small feat.

Most No-Hitters by Franchise through 2014 season

Los Angeles Dodgers (25)
Boston Red Sox (18)
Chicago White Sox (18)
Cincinnati Reds (16)
San Francisco Giants (16)

Most No-Hitters Against

Philadelphia Phillies (19)
Los Angeles Dodgers (18)
Atlanta Braves (17)
San Francisco Giants (16)
Baltimore Orioles/Detroit Tigers/Oakland Athletics (14)

The Padres made it to the playoffs **5** times, but they have never won the World Series.

TRIVIA

1. Which lifelong Padres player batted over .300 in 19 of his 20 seasons, including a mark of .394 in 1994?

2. Which 2 teams defeated the Padres in their 2 World Series appearances?

RIDING THE CYCLE

The Padres have also failed to achieve an offensive milestone that, over the course of baseball history, has occurred about as often as a no-hitter—hitting for the cycle, where a single player hits a single, a double, a triple, and a home run in the same game. Through the end of the 2014 season, 305 players had hit for the cycle. Of baseball's 30 franchises, the Miami Marlins are the only one besides the Padres who have never had a player hit for the cycle.

Most Cycles by Franchise through 2014 Season:

San Francisco Giants (23)

Pittsburgh Pirates (23)

Boston Red Sox (20)

St. Louis Cardinals (19)

Oakland Athletics (17)

COLORADO ROCKIES
★ IT'S OFFENSIVE ★

The Rockies play their home games at Coors Field. Because of a combination of its dimensions (one of the game's vastest outfields) and environmental factors (it sits 5,277 feet above sea level), the ballpark has been one of the game's most offense-friendly since it opened in 1995. Between 1996 and 2001 the Rockies plated more than 900 runs in every season except 1. On May 5, 1999, they also became 1 of just 13 teams in baseball history to score a run in each inning of a game. They did so, however, on the road (at Chicago's Wrigley Field) rather than at Coors Field.

Coors Field has been one of the game's most offense-friendly stadiums since it opened in 1995.

TRIVIA

1. The Rockies were one of 2 expansion teams added to the National League in 1991. What was the other?

2. Which career-long Rockies player holds the team records for home runs, runs batted in, doubles, and walks?

FIELD NOTES

As opposed to a football field or basketball court, the dimensions of the baseball field are only partially standardized. Each ballpark has its share of unique touches, whether the 37-foot-tall Green Monster wall in left field at Boston's Fenway Park or the Tal's Hill incline and flagpole that sits near the wall in center field in Houston's Minute Maid Park. So while teams have a large say over where to position the outfield fences, here are the dimensions that must remain the same in every Major League park:

60 feet, 6 inches
the distance between the pitching rubber and home plate

90 feet
the distance between each of the 4 consecutive bases

15 inches by 15 inches
the size of first, second, and third bases

127 feet, 3.375 inches
the distance between first base and third base as well as between second base and home plate

5 feet in diameter
the size of the on-deck circles

24 inches by 6 inches
the size of the pitching rubber

ARIZONA DIAMONDBACKS

★ ON THE FAST TRACK ★

The Arizona Diamondbacks franchise didn't exist until March 1995 and didn't play its first game until 1998. But improbably, the team made it to the playoffs in its second season. And there they were in November 2001, celebrating a World Series championship after beating the New York Yankees in a 7-game classic.

The series was notable for its mood swings. Even after losing 2 games—on back-to-back nights, no less—in which they had leads in the ninth inning, the Diamondbacks still managed to fight back. In Game 7 they reversed the script, rallying for 2 runs to overcome a ninth-inning deficit. The team has won intermittantly since then, collecting 3 more NL West titles.

The Diamondbacks won 3 NL West titles since winning the World Series in their fourth season.

TRIVIA

1. How old was Randy Johnson when he threw a perfect game against the Braves on May 18, 2004, becoming the oldest pitcher to do so?

2. Which Diamondbacks player holds the franchise record for home runs and runs batted in, as well as the single-season team record for home runs?

THE BOYS OF
SPRING, SUMMER, AND FALL

MLB teams prepare themselves for the season ahead during spring training, a 7-week period of drills and games that starts in mid-February. Currently 15 of the league's 30 teams train in the state of Arizona, playing games in the so-called Cactus League. The other 15 teams train in Florida and play in the Grapefruit League.

Other important dates on the MLB calendar include:

Early April
Start of regular season

Early June
MLB player draft (runs 3 days)

Second or Third Week of July
The All-Star Break (a 4-day break starting on Monday and ending on Thursday, with the All-Star Game played on Tuesday)

July 31
Trade deadline

August 31
Postseason eligibility deadline

Early October
Postseason begins

DEREK JETER'S CAREER STATISTICS

REGULAR SEASON

YEAR	AT-BATS	AVG	OBP	SLG	RUNS	HR	RBI	SB
1995	48	.250	.294	.375	5	0	7	0
1996	582	.314	.370	.430	104	10	78	14
1997	654	.291	.370	.405	116	10	70	23
1998	626	.324	.384	.481	127	19	84	30
1999	627	.349	.438	.552	134	24	102	19
2000	593	.339	.416	.481	119	15	73	22
2001	614	.311	.377	.480	110	21	74	27
2002	644	.297	.373	.421	124	18	75	32
2003	482	.324	.393	.450	87	10	52	11
2004	643	.292	.352	.471	111	23	78	23
2005	654	.309	.389	.450	122	19	70	14
2006	623	.343	.417	.483	118	14	97	34
2007	639	.322	.388	.452	102	12	73	15
2008	596	.300	.363	.408	88	11	69	11
2009	634	.334	.406	.465	107	18	66	30
2010	663	.270	.340	.370	111	10	67	18
2011	546	.297	.355	.388	84	6	61	16
2012	683	.316	.362	.429	99	15	58	9
2013	63	.190	.288	.254	8	1	7	0
2014	581	.256	.304	.313	47	4	50	10
TOTAL	**11,195**	**.310**	**.377**	**.440**	**1,923**	**260**	**1,311**	**358**

PLAYOFFS

Growing up, calculating and understanding baseball stats helped me in math class.

YEAR	AT-BATS	AVG	OBP	SLG	RUNS	HR	RBI	SB
1996	61	.361	.409	.459	12	1	3	3
1997	21	.333	.417	.667	6	2	2	1
1998	51	.235	.328	.294	7	0	3	3
1999	48	.375	.434	.542	10	1	4	3
2000	63	.317	.427	.571	13	4	9	1
2001	62	.226	.275	.290	5	1	4	0
2002	16	.500	.526	.875	6	2	3	0
2003	70	.314	.385	.471	10	2	5	2
2004	49	.245	.339	.347	8	1	9	2
2005	21	.333	.348	.619	4	2	5	1
2006	16	.500	.529	.938	4	1	1	0
2007	17	.176	.176	.176	0	0	1	0
2009	64	.344	.432	.563	14	3	6	0
2010	40	.250	.286	.375	2	0	2	1
2011	24	.250	.280	.292	6	0	2	1
2012	27	.333	.379	.444	4	0	2	0
TOTAL	650	.308	.374	.465	111	20	61	18

DEREK JETER'S YANKEE TEAMS

YEAR	REGULAR-SEASON RECORD
1995	79–65 (2nd in AL East)
1996	92–70 (won AL East)
1997	96–66 (2nd in AL East)
1998	114–48 (won AL East)
1999	98–64 (won AL East)
2000	87–74 (won AL East)
2001	95–65 (won AL East)
2002	103–58 (won AL East)
2003	101–61 (won AL East)
2004	101–61 (won AL East)
2005	95–67 (won AL East)
2006	97–65 (won AL East)
2007	94–68 (2nd in AL East)
2008	89–73 (3rd in AL East)
2009	103–59 (won AL East)
2010	95–67 (2nd in AL East)
2011	97–65 (won AL East)
2012	95–67 (won AL East)
2013	85–77 (3rd in AL East)
2014	84–78 (2nd in AL East)

YEAR	PLAYOFFS
1995	Lost ALDS 3–2 (Seattle Mariners)
1996	Won ALDS 3–1 (Texas Rangers), won ALCS 4–1 (Baltimore Orioles), won WS 4–2 (Atlanta Braves)
1997	Lost ALDS 3–2 (Cleveland Indians)
1998	Won ALDS 3–0 (Texas Rangers), won ALCS 4–2 (Cleveland Indians), won WS 4–0 (San Diego Padres)
1999	Won ALDS 3–0 (Texas Rangers), won ALCS 4–1 (Boston Red Sox), won WS 4–0 (Atlanta Braves)
2000	Won ALDS 3–2 (Oakland A's), won ALCS 4–2 (Seattle Mariners), won WS 4–1 (New York Mets)
2001	Won ALDS 3–2 (Oakland A's), won ALCS 4–1 (Seattle Mariners), lost WS 4–3 (Arizona Diamondbacks)
2002	Lost ALDS 3–1 (Anaheim Angels)
2003	Won ALDS 3–1 (Minnesota Twins), won ALCS 4–3 (Boston Red Sox), lost WS 4–2 (Florida Marlins)
2004	Won ALDS 3–1 (Minnesota Twins), lost ALCS 4–3 (Boston Red Sox)
2005	Lost ALDS 3–2 (Los Angeles Angels of Anaheim)
2006	Lost ALDS 3–1 (Detroit Tigers)
2007	Lost ALDS 3–1 (Cleveland Indians)
2008	(did not qualify)
2009	Won ALDS 3–0 (Minnesota Twins), won ALCS 4–2 (Los Angeles Angels of Anaheim), won WS 4–2 (Philadelphia Phillies)
2010	Won ALDS 3–0 (Minnesota Twins), lost ALCS 4–2 (Texas Rangers)
2011	Lost ALDS 3–2 (Detroit Tigers)
2012	Won ALDS 3–2 (Baltimore Orioles), lost ALCS 4–0 (Detroit Tigers)
2013	(did not qualify)
2014	(did not qualify)

★ BATTER UP ★

SPEND AN EXTRA INNING
WITH
JETER CHILDREN'S PUBLISHING!

VISIT JETERCHILDRENSPUBLISHING.COM
TO LEARN MORE ABOUT JETER CHILDREN'S BOOKS AND DISCOVER GREAT ONLINE ACTIVITIES LIKE THESE:

★ Try a baseball trivia quiz and find out if you are a trivia All-Star.

★ Take a Seventh Inning Stretch with baseball-themed printable activities: word searches, math games, cryptograms, and more!

★ Create your own baseball cards using a downloadable template.

★ Design a gameboard and play "Paper Baseball" using a sheet of paper and a coin.

★ Download educational tools for parents and educators, including curriculum guides and discussion questions.

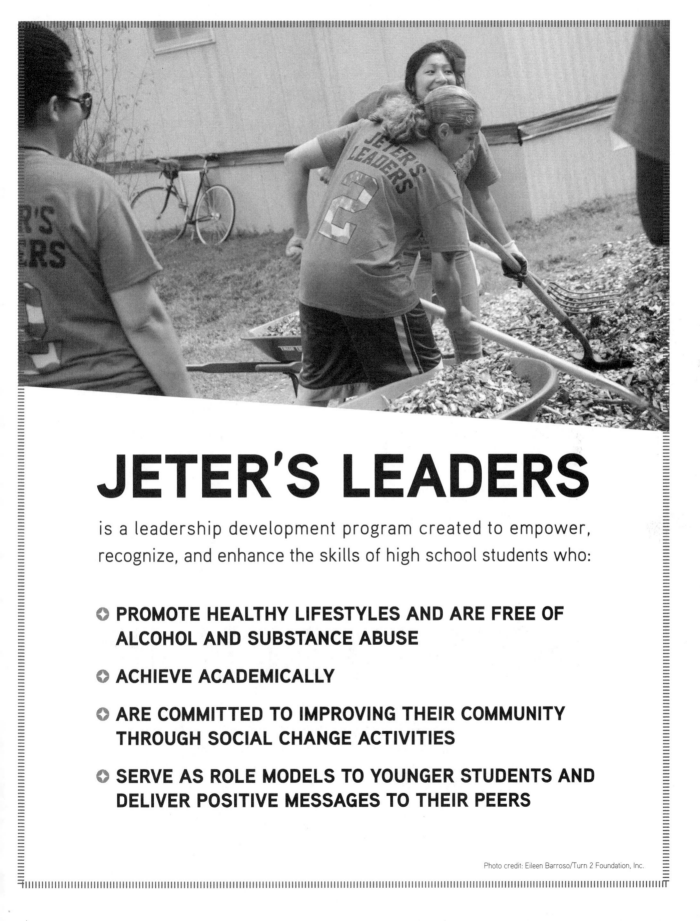

JETER'S LEADERS

is a leadership development program created to empower, recognize, and enhance the skills of high school students who:

- **PROMOTE HEALTHY LIFESTYLES AND ARE FREE OF ALCOHOL AND SUBSTANCE ABUSE**

- **ACHIEVE ACADEMICALLY**

- **ARE COMMITTED TO IMPROVING THEIR COMMUNITY THROUGH SOCIAL CHANGE ACTIVITIES**

- **SERVE AS ROLE MODELS TO YOUNGER STUDENTS AND DELIVER POSITIVE MESSAGES TO THEIR PEERS**

"Your role models should teach you, inspire you, criticize you, and give you structure. My parents did all of these things with their contracts. They tackled every subject. There was nothing we didn't discuss. I didn't love every aspect of it, but I was mature enough to understand that almost everything they talked about made sense." **—DEREK JETER**

DO YOU HAVE WHAT IT TAKES TO BECOME A
JETER'S LEADER?

- I am drug and alcohol free.
- I volunteer in my community.
- I am good to the environment.
- I am a role model for kids.
- I do not use the word "can't."
- I am a role model for my peers and younger kids.
- I stand up for what's right.

- I am respectful to others.
- I encourage others to participate.
- I am open-minded.
- I set my goals high.
- I do well in school.
- I like to exercise and eat well to keep my body strong.
- I am educated on current events.

CREATE A CONTRACT

What are your goals?

Sit down with your parents or an adult mentor to create your own contract to help you take the first step toward achieving your dreams.

For more information on JETER'S LEADERS, visit
TURN2FOUNDATION.ORG